DATE DUE

NO 26 05			

SOUTH AFRICA

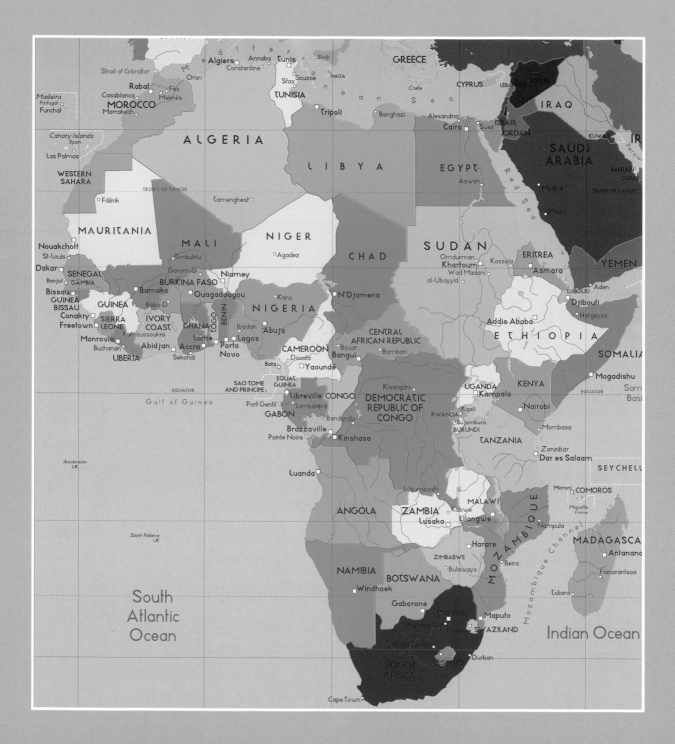

SOUTH AFRICA

Sheila Smith Noonan

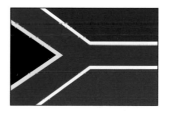

Mason Crest Publishers
Philadelphia

Produced by OTTN Publishing, Stockton, N.J.

Mason Crest Publishers
370 Reed Road
Broomall, PA 19008
www.masoncrest.com

First printing

1 3 5 7 9 8 6 4 2

Library of Congress Cataloging-in-Publication Data

Noonan, Sheila Smith.
  South Africa / Sheila Noonan.
      p. cm. — (Africa)
  Includes bibliographical references and index.
  ISBN 1-59084-819-5
  1. South Africa—Juvenile literature. I. Title. II. Series.

  DT1719.N66 2004
  968--dc22

                                                    2004007102

Africa:
Facts and Figures

Burundi

Democratic Republic
of the Congo

Ethiopia

Ghana

Ivory Coast

Kenya

Nigeria

Rwanda

South Africa

Tanzania

Uganda

Zimbabwe

Table of Contents

Africa: Continent in the Balance

Robert I. Rotberg

Africa is the cradle of humankind, but for millennia it was off the familiar, beaten path of global commerce and discovery. Its many peoples therefore developed largely apart from the diffusion of modern knowledge and the spread of technological innovation until the 17th through 19th centuries. With the coming to Africa of the book, the wheel, the hoe, and the modern rifle and cannon, foreigners also brought the vastly destructive transatlantic slave trade, oppression, discrimination, and onerous colonial rule. Emerging from that crucible of European rule, Africans created nationalistic movements and then claimed their numerous national independences in the 1960s. The result is the world's largest continental assembly of new countries.

There are 53 members of the African Union, a regional political grouping, and 48 of those nations lie south of the Sahara. Fifteen of them, including mighty Ethiopia, are landlocked, making international trade and economic growth that much more arduous and expensive. Access to navigable rivers is limited, natural harbors are few, soils are poor and thin, several countries largely consist of miles and miles of sand, and tropical diseases have sapped the strength and productivity of innumerable millions. Being landlocked, having few resources (although countries along Africa's west coast have tapped into deep offshore petroleum and gas reservoirs), and being beset by malaria, tuberculosis, schistosomiasis, AIDS, and many other maladies has kept much of Africa poor for centuries.

Thirty-two of the world's poorest 44 countries are African. Hunger is common. So is rapid deforestation and desertification. Unemployment rates are often over 50 percent, for jobs are few—even in agriculture. Where Africa once

The independent kingdoms of Lesotho and Swaziland lie within the Republic of South Africa.

was a land of small villages and a few large cities, with almost everyone engaged in growing grain or root crops or grazing cattle, camels, sheep, and goats, today more than half of all the more than 750 million Africans, especially those who live south of the Sahara, reside in towns and cities. Traditional agriculture hardly pays, and a number of countries in Africa—particularly the smaller and more fragile ones—can no longer feed themselves.

There is not one Africa, for the continent is full of contradictions and variety. Of the 675 million people living south of the Sahara, at least 130 million live in Nigeria, 67 million in Ethiopia, 55 million in the Democratic Republic of the

A group of Zulus perform a traditional dance in the KwaZulu-Natal Province.

Congo, and 45 million in South Africa. By contrast, tiny Djibouti and Equatorial Guinea have fewer than 1 million people each, and prosperous Botswana and Namibia each are under 2 million in population. Within some countries, even medium-sized ones like Zambia (11 million), there are a plethora of distinct ethnic groups speaking separate languages. Zambia, typical with its multitude of competing entities, has 70 such peoples, roughly broken down into four language and cultural zones. Three of those languages jostle with English for primacy.

Given the kaleidoscopic quality of African culture and deep-grained poverty, it is no wonder that Africa has developed economically and politically less rapidly than other regions. Since independence from colonial rule, weak governance has also plagued Africa and contributed significantly to the widespread poverty of its peoples. Only Botswana and offshore Mauritius have been governed democratically without interruption since independence. Both are among Africa's wealthiest countries, too, thanks to the steady application of good governance.

Aside from those two nations, and South Africa, Africa has been a continent of coups since 1960, with massive and oil-rich Nigeria suffering incessant periods of harsh, corrupt, autocratic military rule. Nearly every other country on or around the continent, small and large, has been plagued by similar bouts of instability and dictatorial rule. In the 1970s and 1980s Idi Amin ruled Uganda capriciously and Jean-Bedel Bokassa proclaimed himself emperor of the Central African Republic. Macias Nguema of Equatorial Guinea was another in that same mold. More recently Daniel arap Moi held Kenya in thrall and Robert Mugabe has imposed himself on once-prosperous Zimbabwe. In both of those cases, as in the case of Gnassingbe Eyadema in Togo and the late Mobutu Sese Seko in Congo, these presidents stole wildly and drove entire peoples and their nations into penury. Corruption is common in Africa, and so are a weak rule-of-law framework, misplaced development, high expenditures on soldiers and low expenditures on health and education, and a widespread (but not universal) refusal on the part of leaders to work well for their followers and citizens.

Conflict between groups within countries has also been common in Africa. More than 12 million Africans have been killed in the civil wars of Africa since 1990, with more than 3 million losing their lives in Congo and more than 2 million in the Sudan. War between north and south has been constant in the Sudan since 1981. In 2003 there were serious ongoing hostilities in northeastern Congo, Burundi, Angola, Liberia, Guinea, Ivory Coast, the Central African Republic, and Guinea-Bissau, and a coup (later reversed) in São Tomé and Príncipe.

Despite such dangers, despotism, and decay, Africa is improving. Botswana and Mauritius, now joined by South Africa, Senegal, Kenya, and Ghana, are beacons of democratic growth and enlightened rule. Uganda and Senegal are taking the lead in combating and reducing the spread of AIDS, and others are following. There are serious signs of the kinds of progressive economic policy changes that might lead to prosperity for more of Africa's peoples. The trajectory in Africa is positive.

South Africa's beautiful scenery attracts millions of tourists each year. (Opposite) The picturesque Blyde River Canyon stretches 20 miles (33 km) through South Africa's Mpumalanga Province. (Right) Three South African schoolgirls with painted faces smile for a photo on the Eastern Cape.

1 A Postcard-Perfect Land

SAWUBONA! LOTJHANI! BHOTA! Hallo! That's how to say "hello" in Zulu, Ndebele, Xhosa, and Afrikaans—four of South Africa's eleven official languages. Whichever greeting South Africans use, they are happy to welcome visitors to their beautiful *Rainbow Nation*.

Located at the southern tip of the continent, South Africa is aptly named. With an area of 471,010 square miles (1,219,912 square kilometers), the country is about twice the size of Texas and is Africa's seventh-largest country.

South Africa's land neighbors are Namibia to the northwest, Botswana and Zimbabwe to the north, and Mozambique to the northeast. There are also two small independent kingdoms located within South Africa, Swaziland (which shares a border with Mozambique) and Lesotho. Two of the earth's great oceans form a water border with South Africa: the Indian Ocean to the

11

east and south, and the Atlantic Ocean on the west. South Africa's Marion and Prince Edward Islands are in the southern Indian Ocean, about 1,200 miles (1,931 km) from the city of Cape Town.

South Africa has four main geographic regions. Following a "V" shape, there's an outermost, narrow band of coastline known as the lowveld (*veld* is the Afrikaans word for "bush"). The first inland region from the coast is the Great Escarpment, of which the Drakensberg Mountains comprise a large section. Farther toward the interior is the high plateau region, which is dominated by the highveld. The land here rises into the Witwatersrand, a rocky ridge that contains the largest known gold deposits in the world. Finally, the southern basin of the Kalahari Desert reaches the interior from South Africa's northern border.

Climate

Sunny days easily outnumber rainy ones in South Africa. On average, the country receives only about 18 inches of rainfall a year. The lack of rain will often take its toll on South Africa, creating **drought** conditions. Without adequate rainfall, farmers can't grow important crops such as corn and sugar cane. Consequently, livestock and people face the possibility of starvation. In 2003, South Africa experienced one of its worst droughts in more than 80 years.

Although the lack of rainfall can have serious consequences, South Africa's moderate, sunny weather generally makes it a pleasant place to live. Summer extends from September to April, with average temperatures ranging between 66°F and 72°F (19°C and 22°C). The Province of KwaZulu-Natal, located along the eastern coast of South Africa, is known for its humid summer climate. During the winter months (May to August), the weather is cooler in Gauteng, located in the highveld, with average temperatures between 54°F and 62°F (12°C and 17°C).

Swimmers flock to South Africa's eastern and southern coasts, where a tropical current warms the Indian Ocean. The waters of the Atlantic Ocean on the western side are sharply colder because of the Benguela current, which originates from Antarctica. Marine life thrives in these waters, making the west coast the best place to fish in South Africa.

A Natural Beauty

From rolling grasslands to majestic mountains to sandy beaches, South Africa has an abundance of postcard-perfect countryside to explore. South Africa's highest mountain range is the Drakensberg (also known as the Barrier of Spears). Located in KwaZulu-Natal, the peaks of these mountains reach 10,826 feet (3,300 meters). Toward the south, the famous flat-topped Table Mountain overlooks Cape Town. The pretty Garden Route, which stretches for about 485 miles (780 kilometers) along the Western Cape coastline, is a popular driving tour for visitors and South Africans alike. It passes by lovely seaside towns, such as Mossel Bay, where explorer Bartholomeu Dias landed as the first European to reach South Africa. At Tsitsikamma National Park, visitors look up at Giant Yellowwood trees, which can grow as high as 131 feet (40 meters) tall, or go underground to Cango Caves, world famous for their large stalagmite formations.

South Africa's longest interior waterway is the Orange River, also

Quick Facts: The Geography of South Africa

Location: Southern Africa, at the southern tip of the continent of Africa

Area: (slightly less than twice the size of Texas)
  total: 470,886 square miles (1,219,912 sq km)
  land: 470,886 square miles (1,219,912 sq km)
  water: 0 square miles

Borders: Botswana, 1,143 miles (1,840 km); Lesotho, 565 miles (909 km); Mozambique, 305 miles (491 km); Namibia, 305 miles (967 km); Swaziland, 267 miles (430 km); Zimbabwe, 140 miles (225 km); coastline, 1,739 miles (2,798 km)

Climate: mostly semiarid; subtropical along east coast; sunny days, cool nights

Terrain: vast interior plateau rimmed by rugged hills and narrow coastal plain

Elevation extremes:
  lowest point: Atlantic Ocean, 0 feet
  highest point: Njesuthi, 11,181 feet (3,408 meters)

Natural hazards: prolonged droughts

Source: CIA World Factbook, 2003.

known as the Gariep River. It runs for 1,400 miles (2,250 kilometers) from the Free State Province westward until it reaches the Atlantic Ocean. The river's Augrabies Falls is the world's sixth-largest waterfall, cascading down 479 feet (146 meters).

The Western Cape's Great Karoo, a plateau basin, lives up to its indigenous name (*Karoo* means "dry thirst land"). For those fascinated with the distant past, the fossil-filled desert land of the Great Karoo also offers a glimpse of what the earth was like during prehistoric times. About 280 million years ago, the Great Karoo was a giant swamp; today, it is a treasure trove for archaeologists and fossil hunters. It is also home to more than 9,000 species of plants and many birds and animals, including the endangered riverine rabbit and the black rhinoceros.

Unlike the rest of South Africa, Prince Edward and Marion Islands rarely experience sunny days. Snow and rain are the norm, and the Roaring Forties, strong, westerly winds, make it difficult for plants and trees to grow. Both islands were formed by volcanic activity, and in 1980 the volcano on Marion Island erupted. While the islands don't adequately support most forms of life, their shores are home to king penguins and elephant seals.

An afternoon view of Augrabies Falls, which drops 627 feet (191 meters), making it the world's sixth-highest waterfall. Augrabies Falls is located in a national park in the Northern Cape.

Beasts, Birds, and Blossoms

The most spine-tingling attractions in South Africa are the natural ones. The possibility of catching a glimpse of lions, hippos, and ostriches in the wild draws hundreds of thousands of visitors to South Africa every year. The country is best known for its "Big Five" wildlife—elephants, lions, rhinos, leopards, and buffalo—but there is much more to see. Kruger National Park, located in the northeast province of Eastern Transvaal, is home to the Big Five as well as wildebeest, antelope, hyenas, and about 127 other mammals. There are also more than 100 types of reptiles, nearly 500 different species of birds, and 300 kinds of trees. In contrast to this great diversity, the arid climate and red sand dunes of the Northern Cape's Kalahari Gemsbok National Park provide a habitat for only a few species. These species, most of which are rare, include the gemsbok (a member of the antelope family), meerkat, bat-eared fox, Kalahari lion, and the park's main attraction, the cheetah.

Among South Africa's biggest challenges is finding ways to protect its wildlife. The practice of bringing home "trophy" animals from safari hunts has threatened the populations of certain species. Farming, mining, and urban development also have taken their toll on land that once readily provided food and habitat for the animals. Naturalists are especially concerned about the cheetah, which farmers often shoot because they eat the livestock. In December 2003, the *Mail & Guardian* newspaper reported that fewer than 1,000 of these shy, speedy big cats remain in the country. As a solution to this problem, some organizations have paid farmers a reward for safely capturing live cheetah, after which the conservationists relocate the troublesome cats.

Animals aren't the only natural wonders in South Africa. The Cape Floral Kingdom, one of six distinct botanical regions in the world, is located primarily in the Western Cape. There are about 8,500 floral species growing within an area of 17,760 square miles (45,998 sq km)—about twice the size of New Jersey. The kingdom is famous for its tough-leaved Fynbos plants, and the king protea, a kind of Fynbos plant and South Africa's national flower, is not found anywhere else in the world.

A herd of elephants wanders into a river in Kruger National Park. The park is the oldest nature reserve in Africa. It was established in 1898 by the president of the South African Republic, Paul Kruger, and later renamed in his honor.

South Africa's history stretches back thousands of years. (Opposite) Early South African inhabitants lived in the Karoo region, which is now a national garden and park. (Right) A San hunter takes aim at a possible target. The San are believed to have lived in South Africa for about 20,000 years.

2 Troubling Past, Promising Future

SOUTH AFRICA'S EARLIEST history began in the first millennium B.C., when peoples living on the African continent arrived to settle in the south. The San (Bushmen) hunters made their homes in the rugged Drakensberg mountains and desertlike Karoo region; the Khoikhoi took to the southern plains; and agro-pastoralists—farmers and livestock herders—settled in the east near what is now the KwaZulu-Natal Province.

By about A.D. 1250, the agro-pastoralists had settled most of the eastern half of present-day South Africa. The Khoikhoi and the agro-pastoralists had formed chiefdoms. The San organized into smaller, family-based groupings, and thus had simpler political structures than their farming and herding neighbors had.

Although there was plenty of contact between the different groups, the land that would become South Africa remained fairly isolated from the rest of the world. When the Europeans arrived, they encountered a society that was divided in many different ways. This division would prove to be a challenge when they began colonizing in the mid-17th century.

The White Settlers

The explorers of the 15th and later centuries were primarily motivated by trade and the routes that would best facilitate it. When Portuguese explorer Bartholomeu Dias rounded what was later named the Cape of Good Hope in 1488, he only believed his discovery was the opening of a new sea route.

Europeans didn't consider this cape more than a trading stop until 1652, when the Dutch East India Tea Company formed a colony there. At first, the Dutchmen traded goods with the Khoikhoi for food and water. When this arrangement didn't work out, the Dutch decided that they needed to settle permanently for their businesses to survive. But the Khoikhoi were not willing to give their land to the whites, and thus began many years of fighting between whites and the tribes. Although the Khoikhoi fought back as best they could, the whites had the advantage of firearms.

By the end of the 1600s, the Dutch brought in slaves from West Africa, India, and the Indonesian island of Java. Groups of Dutch, French, and German people also arrived to work the land as migrant farmers. They constantly wanted to acquire more land, which meant waging war with the Khoikhoi. Upon facing their better-armed opponents, the Khoikhoi soon realized they had two life-sparing options: move off their land or work on the farms and pastures of the settlers. During one tragic period in Khoikhoi his-

This promontory jutting into the Atlantic Ocean was originally dubbed the "Cape of Storms" by Portuguese explorer Bartholomeu Dias, who sighted it in 1488. The landmark was renamed the Cape of Good Hope by King John II of Portugal. The new name signified Portuguese hopes for the sea route around Africa that they hoped would allow them to trade with India, China, East Africa, and the islands of the Indian Ocean.

tory even staying alive was a challenge, because around 1713, a smallpox epidemic swept through Cape Town that resulted in the deaths of nearly 90 percent of the Khoikhoi population.

The British arrived to Cape Town in small numbers in the late 1700s, briefly occupying the colony before turning it back over to the Dutch in 1803. In 1814, Great Britain regained control of the Cape Colony as part of a treaty that ended the Napoleonic Wars. These were a series of conflicts fought by the British and various European countries against France, which was ruled by Napoleon Bonaparte. Soon after the wars ended, many British journeyed to South Africa. Because the colony was governed by British law, the trading of slaves ended in 1834, as it had been abolished throughout the empire.

Even as the Napoleonic Wars raged, another military force had been rising to prominence far to the northeast of Cape Town. These were the Zulu, a tribe of cattle herders and farmers. Under Shaka Zulu, a legendary warrior and the tribe's king, the Zulu reached their peak in the early 1800s. Shaka was adept at consolidating neighboring tribes of similar language and background. Through their great numbers and common agenda, the Zulu gained political power and military might. Shaka was murdered by his half-brothers in 1828, but he remains highly revered among the Zulus and is one of the most famous figures of South African history.

Like the Dutch, the British fought with tribespeople over land. For several decades, they engaged in frontier wars with the Xhosa tribe, mighty opponents who at times scored surprise victories over the British. By about 1853, however, there were only small pockets of Xhosa resistance.

The Great Trek and the Boer Wars

By the 1830s many of the Dutch were unhappy with English rule. After settling in South Africa they had developed a distinctive culture and language called *Afrikaans*, which is similar to Dutch. Their values stemmed from their Christian sect, the Dutch Reformed Church. This church preached that God chose them to be a special people and had important plans for them, which included asserting their superiority over black Africans. When Britain decided to end the slave trade, the Afrikaners were disgruntled as expected.

The settlers also desired land on which to graze their cattle, and in 1835 they began to move north and northeast of the Cape Colony in search of land to claim. About 10,000 *Voortrekkers* (Afrikaans for "those who move ahead") embarked on what became known as the Great Trek. Many of these migrants were semi-nomadic pastoral farmers called *trekboers*, from whom the Boers later derived their name. During their journey they met with resistance from the people whose land they were trying to take, the Ndebele and the Zulu. The Voortrekkers believed God would give them victory over the tribes; that conviction only grew stronger after they won a battle on December 16, 1838, in which 464 Voortrekkers defeated more than 10,000 Zulu warriors. About 3,000 Zulus died in that skirmish, known as the Battle of Blood River, yet no Voortrekkers were killed. From that point on, the Voortrekkers, or Afrikaners, as they became known, set up their own republics of the Orange Free State and the Transvaal.

Tensions between the Afrikaners and the British only increased in 1869 when diamonds were discovered in the Transvaal outpost of Kimberley. To gain control of diamond mining in the area, Britain annexed the Transvaal in 1877, but just four years later the Afrikaners soundly defeated the British in the Battle of Majuba Hill. In the resulting treaty, signed in Pretoria, the British granted the Afrikaners independence. The

These bronze cannons and covered wagons mark the location of the Battle of Blood River. During this 1838 battle, a handful of Voortrekkers defeated a large army of Zulu warriors.

new country was named the South African Republic, and Paul Kruger became its first elected president in 1883.

When gold was found in the Transvaal hills in 1886, it wasn't long before the British once again tried to take over the land. British settlers gradually infiltrated the region, and under Leander Starr Jameson they banned together to launch a rebellion against the South African Republic in 1895. This rebellion was not officially ordered by Britain, though it indicated that the British-Afrikaner conflict was still unresolved, and that there was more fighting to come. To safeguard their independence, the South African Republic and the Orange Free State formed a military alliance in 1896.

The Anglo-Boer War, also known as the South African War, began in 1899 and ended in 1902. Although the Afrikaners won early military victories, the British came back strongly and took over Johannesburg and Pretoria. Just when the British thought they had the upper hand, the Afrikaners began using guerrilla-style attacks. The British fought back ruthlessly, burning farms and killing civilians to root out the Afrikaner fighters, as well as establishing concentration camps for women and children. Before the Afrikaners had conceded defeat, there were more civilian casualties of the war than deaths of British and Afrikaner soldiers combined.

New Leadership, Old Prejudice

By 1910, the colonial period of South Africa's history had ended. The Act of Union, a law passed by the British parliament, created the self-governing Union of South Africa, though technically it was still part of the British Commonwealth.

The Union had four provinces: the Cape of Good Hope, Transvaal, the Orange Free State, and Natal. Its first prime minister was Louis Botha, a Boer War general who believed that the British and Afrikaner South Africans could settle their differences.

Although a new leadership was put in place, the old attitude toward blacks remained entrenched. A series of laws was passed by an all-white parliament that chipped away at the rights of blacks. Under the Mines and Works Acts of 1911 and 1926, for example, jobs were assigned on the basis of skin color, and whites received higher wages than blacks. In 1913, the Natives Land Act restricted blacks (who were, by far, the numerical majority) to 13 percent of the land, leaving the remaining 87 percent of the land to whites. Under the Natives (Urban Areas) Act of 1923, blacks were forced to carry special identification papers when they were in a city.

Non-white South Africans established an organized resistance to racist legislation. As early as 1909, the Indian pacifist leader Mohandas Gandhi, who was living in South Africa at the time, organized demonstrations and labor strikes. When several of South Africa's influential blacks became aware that the Natives Land Act was about to be legislated in 1912, they formed the South African Native National Congress to address racial inequality. In 1923, the group changed its name to the African National Congress (ANC) and committed itself to opposing the discriminatory laws. By the end of the 1940s, two other ANC organizations were established: the ANC Women's League, and the ANC Youth League, founded by Nelson Mandela, Walter Sisulu, and other leaders.

There were several forces making government policy racially divisive. One secret but influential group espousing Afrikaner nationalism and racial inequality was the Afrikaner Broederbond (League of Afrikan Brothers). Formed in 1918, this group grew more politically powerful over succeeding decades. By 1948, the year that the Afrikaners' National Party won the national election, the Broederbond had developed extreme segregationist views among pro-fascist Afrikaners. The group's impact on South African politics would be felt for years to come.

Under the leadership of the new prime minister, Daniel Malan, *apartheid* became official policy. *Apartheid*, the Afrikaans word for "separate," was a system of racial segregation and white supremacy. In 1950, the Population Registration Act required all South Africans to register with the government and be classified as one of four groups: white, black, Colored (people of mixed black and white ances-try), or Indian. Blacks were issued so-called **pass books** that contained their fingerprints, picture, and racial identifi-cation. They had to present their pass books to enter a "non-black" area as determined by another 1950 law, the Group Areas Act.

Another critical piece of National Party legislation was the Bantu Education Act, passed in 1953. This act established an educational system that segregated the schools and provided two basic types of learning opportunities. White children were taught to read, write, and do mathematics on levels that would prepare them for college. Black children were placed in schools with few resources and not enough teachers. Their instruction only prepared them for low-level jobs. If non-white children wanted to go to college, a 1959 law prohibited them from attending a white university unless they had special permission from the government. While attending black

South Africa's policy of apartheid was officially implemented in 1948. Blacks and whites had been segregated in the preceding decades, and remained segregated for several more decades. In this 1976 photo, a sign written in English and Afrikaans denotes a "whites only" area of the beach near Cape Town.

colleges was an option, these schools did not nearly have the resources or status that white universities had.

As apartheid policy grew worse, the resistance movement expanded and gained strength. In 1952, South Africans of all races (including some whites) participated in a campaign to protest the unfair legislation. Finding power in their numbers, they deliberately broke pass laws and other rules so they would be arrested and overflow the jails. Three years later, the ANC, the Indian National Congress, the Coloured People's Organisation, and other groups drew up the Freedom Charter, a document promoting equal rights for *all* South Africans. Thinking that its plans were threatened by the charter, the

African National Congress Youth League founders Nelson Mandela (left) and Walter Sisulu speak together in the Robben Island prison yard in 1965. Two years earlier the two men had been arrested, tried for treason, and sentenced to life imprisonment.

government charged many of the resistance leaders with *treason*; however, it could not make a convincing argument and by 1961 all of the accused were found not guilty.

Apartheid in Full Swing

By 1960, the National Party's plan to essentially create two South Africas was moving forward. Blacks and other people of color had low-paying jobs (if they were employed at all) and lived in shoddy housing, often on the outskirts of cities and towns where white people had decent homes. These black settlements became known as *townships*. The government even built dormitory-style housing for blacks near white areas so that there would be a pool of low-skilled workers from which to draw.

During this time, blacks were still required to carry pass books. On March 21, 1960, between 5,000 and 7,000 blacks staged a peaceful protest in the township of Sharpeville. They flooded the police station, offering to be arrested. The police reacted by shooting at the crowd, killing 69 people and injuring many others. The Sharpeville Massacre, as it became known, made the South African government fearful of any mass gathering of blacks. Several organizations, including the ANC, were banned by the government and were forced underground. The massacre also signaled a transition in the ANC's history. From that point on, the organization was willing to resort to violence. The Umkhonto we Sizwe (Spear of the Nation) became the ANC's military arm.

After the Sharpeville Massacre, South Africa came under heavy criticism by other countries and the United Nations for its apartheid policy.

Dead and wounded blacks lie in the streets of Sharpeville, where peaceful anti-apartheid demonstrators were shot by police, killing 69.

Rather than let his country be forced out of the British Commonwealth, Prime Minister Hendrik Verwoerd decided to hold a national vote on whether South Africa should leave of its own accord. It was not a fair election: blacks, Indians, and Coloreds were not allowed to vote. By a margin of about 75,000 votes, South Africa left the Commonwealth and became the Republic of South Africa. On May 31, 1961, South Africa officially cut its ties with Great Britain.

The early 1960s saw the beginning of Umkhonto we Sizwe's military activity, with many acts of sabotage. In 1963, South African officials arrested many ANC leaders at Liliesleaf farm in Rivonia. In what became known as the Rivonia Treason Trial, held a year later, eight leaders—including Walter Sisulu and Nelson Mandela—received life imprisonment sentences.

At the turn of the decade, the South African government passed the Bantu Homelands Citizens Act of 1970, which further developed a decade-old program of pushing black South Africans into segregated residential zones. Blacks were forced to live in one of ten "homeland" districts that had been established in the country's most remote areas. They not only lost their homes, but their South African citizenship was taken from them as well. By default, they had become citizens of one of ten homelands with their own flags and virtually powerless legislatures.

The National Party's white supremacy policies and laws only led to more protests—both peaceful and violent—by the underground ANC and other banned groups. One peaceful protest by students in 1976 is now known as the

An aerial view shows the confusion of the Soweto riots in June 1976. Hundreds of blacks were killed in the riots, which started after South African police attacked a large crowd of peaceful schoolchildren.

Soweto uprising. Soweto, an acronym for Southwest African Township, was a fledgling community on the outskirts of Johannesburg (it is now a major city). On June 16, 1976, about 20,000 schoolchildren began a peaceful march protesting the educational system's policy of teaching in Afrikaans. The police fired tear gas and the bullets at the crowd, sparking a massive riot that lasted for weeks and claimed the lives of hundreds of black youths. South Africa had already grown isolated from the rest of the world, but the Soweto riots resulted in even more *economic sanctions* against the country.

One year later, resistance leader Stephen Biko was apprehended at a police roadblock. While in custody, Biko suffered massive brain injuries, the result of police brutality, and died en route to a prison. He became the most well-known martyr of the anti-apartheid movement.

A Return to Democracy

Conflict between South African blacks and whites continued throughout the late 1970s and the 1980s. International sanctions remained in place, too, hurting South Africa's economy. World leaders shunned the South African government, and the country's athletes were not allowed to participate in international sporting events like the Olympics.

While the ANC and other groups agitated in the political arena and on the streets, the government faced pressure from another organization—the church. No account of anti-apartheid history is complete without mentioning Desmond Tutu, a priest who rose to become Archbishop of Cape Town, the highest title in the South African Anglican Church. Bishop Tutu used his honored position to speak forcefully against apartheid, even calling for other nations to impose economic sanctions against his own country. He received the Nobel Peace Prize in 1984.

Prime Minister P. W. Botha, a National Party member who took a moderate stance against apartheid, led South Africa from 1978 to 1989. He tried to gain the support of Coloreds and Indians by establishing a tricameral parliament, in which each ethnic group had its own separate legislature. His efforts were unsuccessful because the whites in Parliament still had more seats than the Colored and Indians combined. In 1984, the United Democratic Front, an umbrella anti-apartheid group, organized a highly effective boycott of the national elections, which let Indians and Colored participate in government but not blacks.

Botha's successor, F. W. de Klerk, went further to acknowledge that apartheid was dividing and hurting South Africa. Soon after his election in September 1989, de Klerk lifted the prohibition against the ANC and 32 other organizations. He also authorized the release of several political prisoners, including Nelson Mandela, who had been in prison for 27 years.

In the early 1990s, efforts were underway to build a South African government committed to national unity. Apartheid laws were stricken from the books, one by one. The dream of a free vote and a multiparty government was becoming reality. In April 1994, South Africa held its first democratic elections. Nelson Mandela was elected president, and de Klerk and Thabo Mbeki became deputy presidents.

Mandela was faced with the cumbersome challenge of rebuilding a racially fragmented and economically weakened country. One of the first steps toward South Africa's reconstruction was the Truth and

Archbishop Desmond Tutu (left) was a leader in the fight against apartheid; in 1984 he received the Nobel Peace Prize for his work. In this March 2003 photo he hands the final report of South Africa's Truth and Reconciliation Commission (TRC) to Thabo Mbeki, president of South Africa. The TRC was established to help South Africans deal with the violence and human rights abuses that occurred while the country was under the apartheid system.

Reconciliation Commission, established in 1996 to investigate apartheid-related crimes. *Amnesty* was given to people who confessed to politically motivated crimes. In its final report, the commission documented 22,000

South Africans who said they had been victims of apartheid crimes. Of the 7,000 people who applied for amnesty, 1,200 were accepted. The new South African government has also tried to strengthen the economy through various reforms, though high levels of inflation and unemployment have remained major obstacles.

Mandela's term as president lasted until 1999. That year his deputy president and choice for his successor, Thabo Mbeki, became president, and the ANC maintained its overwhelming majority in the legislature. The Mbeki administration tried to solve some of South Africa's most pressing problems, such as crime, unemployment, poverty, and inadequate housing, and during his first term there were promising signs of economic growth. However, Mbeki was widely criticized for his administration's handling of South Africa's biggest public health crisis, the AIDS pandemic.

HIV/AIDS in South Africa

According to South African Department of Health estimates, by the end of 2002, 5.3 million South Africans were infected with HIV (human immunodeficiency virus). HIV causes AIDS (acquired immunodeficiency syndrome), which if untreated makes people very sick and is ultimately fatal.

Some statements Mbeki has made have outraged HIV/AIDS specialists, most notably his claims that the incidence of HIV in his country is exaggerated and that HIV does not cause AIDS (a very dubious claim within the scientific community). What is perhaps more troubling to healthcare professionals is the administration's delayed response in seriously addressing the national crisis. In November 2003, the government finally took some positive

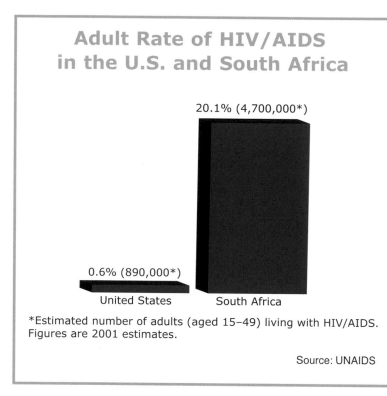

Adult Rate of HIV/AIDS in the U.S. and South Africa

20.1% (4,700,000*)

0.6% (890,000*)

United States   South Africa

*Estimated number of adults (aged 15–49) living with HIV/AIDS. Figures are 2001 estimates.

Source: UNAIDS

action when it introduced the Operational Plan for Comprehensive Treatment and Care for HIV and AIDS. This plan includes the provision of drugs that can treat, though not cure, the disease. It also entails the construction of "service points" in every municipality to provide treatment, awareness, and prevention services related to HIV and AIDS.

End of Apartheid, End of Racism?

Although South Africa began a new era in 1994 with the end of the apartheid system, some people believe the country has yet to truly become the unified nation that the leaders of the freedom movement had envisioned. A 2000 BBC news story reported that a number of rural blacks had been the victims of racially based attacks by white South Africans. In October 2002, a group of white extremists claimed responsibility for bombings in Soweto that killed one woman.

Although these attacks have taken place, there is evidence that racial attitudes are changing in South Africa. In *Public Attitudes in Contemporary South Africa*, a 2001 survey showed that 42 percent of the respondents believed race relations were improving; only 15 percent thought relations were worsening. One of the study's authors, Arlene Grossberg, concluded that "there is good reason to believe that the means to consolidating South Africa's democracy are working."

(Opposite) The illuminated Union Building in Pretoria, where the administrative headquarters of South Africa's government has been located since 1913. (Right) South Africa's president-elect, Nelson Mandela (left), meets with outgoing president F. W. de Klerk, South African Foreign Minister Pik Botha, and Inkatha Freedom Party leader Mangosuthu Buthelezi in April 1994.

3 A Young Republic

THE REPUBLIC OF SOUTH Africa offers people living in the 21st century the unique opportunity to observe the development and growth of a new nation. Following its formative stages in the early 1990s, a democratic South Africa emerged on April 27, 1994, with its first elections open to people of all races. Since then, the world has watched South Africa transform itself from a country of prejudice to one of promise.

The Constitution

South Africa has a democratic system of government. In a democracy, regularly scheduled elections are held, and all adult citizens have the right to vote. Certain rights, such as freedom of speech, are guaranteed in a written constitution. The Constitution of the Republic of South Africa was signed in

39

December 1996 and it went into effect early in 1997. South African leaders worked hard to construct it and their efforts paid off.

The new South African constitution is believed to be among the most progressive in the world. Human rights, for so many years denied to black South Africans, are the document's major focus. The most significant rights now guaranteed to South Africans are the right to an education, freedom of religion, and—perhaps most important—protection against discrimination. To paraphrase the South African constitution's preamble, the new government's goals are to heal the divisions of the past; improve the quality of life for all citizens; set the foundations of a democratic society; and build a united and democratic South Africa.

The Government System

There are three levels of government in South Africa: national, provincial, and local. The national government is responsible for making decisions and laws that affect the entire country and its relationships with other nations; provincial governments oversee the activities of each of the provinces within South Africa; and local governments manage municipalities within the provinces.

The president is head of state and leader of the country's national government. He or she chooses a deputy president and about two dozen ministers to form the presidential cabinet, an assembly that helps the president to govern. Each minister leads departments of the national government, which include education, housing, foreign affairs, and tourism.

South African citizens do not directly elect the president. Instead, they elect members of a branch of Parliament, known as the National Assembly, who then select the president. With as many as 400 members, the National Assembly is more powerful than the other branch of Parliament, the National Council of Provinces. The Assembly's primary responsibility is to make laws. Its subcommittees, called Portfolio Committees, draft legislation that are presented for vote by the full Assembly. It also approves the national budget and keeps deputy ministers accountable by holding weekly question sessions about their departments.

Each of South Africa's nine provinces sends ten delegates to the National Council of Provinces. The delegates represent the legislature of their particular province, in contrast to Assembly members, who are considered more representative of the general populace. Because Assembly members have this direct connection, they have more influence on the legislation that both houses of Parliament pass.

In 1994, South Africa was divided into nine political provinces: Limpopo, Mpumalanga, Gauteng, KwaZulu-Natal, Eastern Cape, Western Cape, Northern Cape, North West, and Free State. Just as each state in the United States has a governor and a legislature, each South African province has a leader—known as a premier—and a lawmaking body.

Much of South Africa's government operations boil down to the local level. South Africa has 284 municipalities that belong to one of three groups: metropolitan (also known as unicities), district, and local. The six unicities—Johannesburg, Cape Town, East Rand, Durban, Pretoria, and Port Elizabeth—are independent, with their own mayors and executive committees. Local municipalities are often part of district municipalities, whose chief responsibility is district-wide planning. SALGA (South African Local Government Association) is a constitutionally created organization that provides research and consulting services to local governments and promotes the new role of local governments.

South Africa recognizes tribal monarchs as the country's traditional leaders and important figures in South African society. Each of the six Provincial Houses of Traditional Leaders send three delegates to the National House of Traditional Leaders, which acts in an advisory capacity to the government. The precise role of village chiefs in the new South African government continues to be debated and refined.

King Goodwill of the Zulu Nation is perhaps the most well-known tribal monarch. In addition to preserving his tribe's values and traditions, he has been vocal about South Africa's most troubling contemporary problem, the fight against HIV/AIDS. In 2004, he called on the United Kingdom and other countries that had taken away land to make *reparations* to the tribes.

Political Parties

In 1994, the African National Congress (ANC), which championed the anti-apartheid cause for decades, came into power. The canvas of a new country was laid before the party, and President Nelson Mandela held the paintbrush. The ANC also dominated the 1999 election, capturing nearly two-thirds of the vote, and the National Assembly selected the new ANC president, Thabo Mbeki, as Mandela's successor.

The ANC is still South Africa's leading political party, but there are many others that have smaller yet significant political voices and appear on the voting ballot in each election. The Democratic Alliance, led by Tony Leon, has been highly critical of the ANC leadership and is the official opposition party. Most members of the Democratic Alliance are white liberals. The Inkatha Freedom Party, formed in the 1920s to preserve Zulu culture, is comprised mostly of Zulus and is led by Mangosuthu Buthelezi. The African Christian Democratic Party bases many of its political goals on Bible teachings and Christian values.

The government of South Africa recognizes tribal rulers, including Chief Buthelezi (left) and King Goodwill Zwelithini (right) of the Zulu. Under this system, traditional forms of leadership are preserved.

The leader of the Democratic Alliance, Tony Leon, smiles and greets supporters during a 2004 election event in Durban.

For a young nation, South Africa is an old hand at "politics as usual," with political alliances forming and ending quickly. For example, a 16-month partnership between the New National Party and the Democratic Party, known as the Democratic Alliance, came to an end in 2001. The New National Party then joined forces with the ANC, forming a "co-operation pact" that was endorsed in 2004 by former National Party leader F. W. de

Klerk. In 2003, the Democratic Alliance kept its old name and formed a new political friendship with the Inkatha Freedom Party in an attempt to take on the ANC.

The ANC's leadership of South Africa was criticized strongly by political opponents in the weeks leading to the 2004 election. Allegations of corruption made some question the government's integrity. Inadequate housing and high levels of unemployment were fuel for the opponents' fire. But perhaps more than any other issue, the Mbeki administration faced unrelenting attack on its HIV/AIDS policy, which critics said was too little and too late to meet the needs of millions of South Africans.

South Africa has a wealth of mineral resources, including gold, copper, iron ore, diamonds, and platinum. (Opposite) An open-pit copper mine in Limpopo. (Right) A South African herdsman tends his cattle as they feed in the Northern Cape.

4 South Africa's Financial Landscape

FROM AN ECONOMIC perspective, South Africa is a country of contrasts. It has many natural resources and is the world's top producer of gold and platinum. However, about 40 percent of South Africans are unemployed. Many people, especially blacks, live in poverty. According to *Breaking the Grip of Poverty and Inequality in South Africa 2004–2014*, a report by a group of South African professors, approximately 40 percent of South Africans live in poverty and the poorest 15 percent are "in a desperate struggle to survive."

The reasons for South Africa's high levels of unemployment and poverty are complex, but it is clear that apartheid has had a negative impact. The Bantu educational system that was implemented in the 1950s provided minimal learning opportunities for blacks, preparing them for only lower-level jobs. Apartheid also led to South Africa's economic isolation. In 1986, the

47

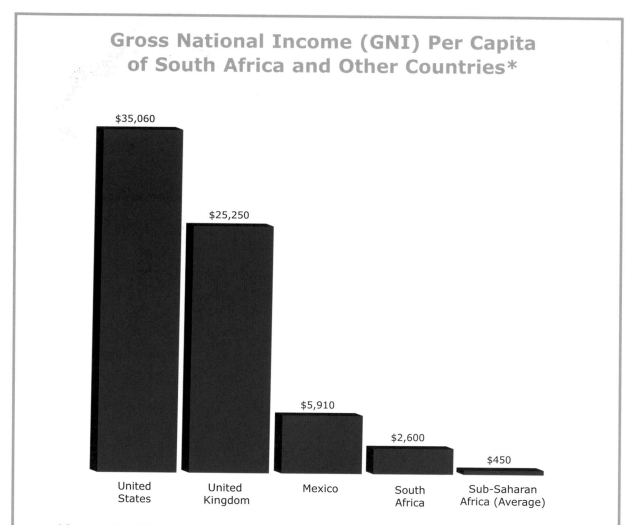

Gross National Income (GNI) Per Capita of South Africa and Other Countries*

United States	$35,060
United Kingdom	$25,250
Mexico	$5,910
South Africa	$2,600
Sub-Saharan Africa (Average)	$450

*Gross national income per capita is the total value of all goods and services produced domestically in a year, supplemented by income received from abroad, divided by midyear population. The above figures take into account fluctuations in currency exchange rates and differences in inflation rates across global economies.

Figures are 2002 estimates. Source: World Bank, 2003.

United States imposed its own economic sanctions against South Africa, prohibiting American companies to make new investments and bank loans.

Even before government sanctions were put in place, many large international corporations like Exxon and Coca-Cola had pulled out of South Africa. Largely because of public pressure, companies and universities withdrew financial investments and stopped trading stocks. The U.S. sanctions against South Africa were lifted in 1991, and since the creation of a democratic South African government, many international companies have resumed doing business in the country. In 2004, General Motors announced it would return after a 17-year absence. The car manufacturer was among the last large companies to resume operations in South Africa.

Improving the national economy is one of the post-apartheid government's top priorities. The government exercised tight control over the economy during the years of apartheid, but post-apartheid policies encourage private investments and competition. Creating jobs is another major objective, which is no easy task in light of the country's high population growth. According to *Breaking the Grip of Poverty and Inequality*, 1.6 million jobs were created between 1995 and 2002, but during that same period, the job market grew by 5 million people. The government and the private sector are trying new strategies to create jobs. For example, the government and organized labor agreed in 2003 to place 72,000 young people in "learnerships"—a type of apprenticeship.

One measure of South Africa's progress is its growth in *gross domestic product (GDP)*—the total value of all the goods and services it produces in a year. South Africa's GDP had climbed by 3.4 percent in 2000, but the rate of growth slowed to 2.2 percent in 2001. Until the value of the South African rand, the country's monetary unit, declined against the dollar in 2001, the government was able to hold the rate of inflation to about 6 percent. However, in 2002, the rate climbed to nearly 10 percent.

The repeal of apartheid policies and passage of key legislation and trade agreements have enabled South Africa to enjoy renewed trading relationships with other countries. The Trade, Development and Cooperation Agreement (TDCA) between South Africa and the European Union is opening export and import markets, with both parties agreeing to lower *duties* on goods. Although the European Union is South Africa's most important trading partner, the United States is also a major player. The African Growth and Opportunity Act (AGOA), signed into law in 2000, provides for duty-free South African exports to the United States. In 2003, top AGOA exports to the United States from South Africa included fruit juices, iron, vehicles, steel, and clothing. South Africa is pursing other trade negotiations with China, India, and Nigeria.

Found and Made in South Africa

With the discovery of diamonds in Kimberley in 1869 and gold in Witwatersrand in 1886, mining soon became South Africa's most important industry. Today, about 40 percent of the world's gold reserves are located in Witwatersrand, and more than 400,000 people work at nearly 700 South African quarries and mines. In addition to gold and diamonds, South Africa is a world-leading producer of platinum, coal, iron ore, uranium, and other minerals. More than one-third of what South Africa earns from exports comes through the sale of mineral products.

While mining is the foundation of the South African economy, farming and food processing still play an important part. Maize (corn), oats, wheat, and sugar cane are the main crops, and cattle and sheep are raised for market. The food industry employs about 450,000 people.

South Africa's information technology (IT) and electronics sector spans the market from cell phones to software. It also is emerging as a major contributor

Quick Facts: The Economy of South Africa

Gross domestic product (GDP*):
$427.7 billion
Inflation: 9.9% (2003 est.)
Economic Growth Rate: 3%
Natural Resources: gold, chromium, antimony, coal, iron ore, manganese, nickel, phosphates, tin, uranium, gem diamonds, platinum, copper, vanadium, salt, natural gas
Agriculture (4.4% of GDP): corn, wheat, sugarcane, fruits, vegetables; beef, poultry, mutton, wool, dairy products (2001 est.)
Industry (28.9% of GDP): mining (world's largest producer of platinum, gold, chromium), automobile assembly, metalworking, machinery, textile, iron and steel, chemicals, fertilizer, foodstuffs (2001 est.)
Services (66.7% of GDP): government, other (2001 est.)

Foreign Trade:
Exports–$31.8 billion: gold, diamonds, platinum, other metals and minerals, machinery and equipment (1998 est.)
Imports–$29.7 billion: machinery and equipment, chemicals, petroleum products, scientific instruments, foodstuffs (2000 est.)
Currency Exchange Rate: U.S. $1 = 6.33 rands (2004)

*GDP, or gross domestic product, is the total value of goods and services produced in a country annually.
All figures are 2002 estimates unless otherwise indicated.
Sources: CIA World Factbook, 2003; Bloomberg.com.

Tourism is South Africa's fourth-largest industry; the country's scenery and wildlife attract about 6.5 million visitors each year. (Left) Tourists take photos of an elephant. (Bottom) Table Mountain, which rises 3,563 feet (1,086 meters) above sea level, is a famous landmark. Many adventurers hike to the summit to see the thousands of different wildflower species that grow there.

to the South African economy, with telecommunications alone accounting for more than 7 percent of the GDP. Some enterprising South Africans are using technology to expand their businesses far beyond the continent. The country's financial services also show healthy growth. Banks, mortgage companies, insurance firms, and investment organizations serve domestic and international markets.

With nearly 6.5 million visitors a year (about 1 million annually to Kruger National Park), tourism has proven to be an indispensable industry for South Africa. About 25 percent of the tourists are from Europe, and nearly 10 percent come from North America. The tourism sector, which includes restaurants, hotel, and tourist attractions, employs about 7 percent of South Africa's workers and is the country's fourth-largest industry.

(Opposite) A Zulu man holding a shield and spear stands outside his house in the KwaZulu-Natal Province. While many South Africans enjoy a modern lifestyle, tribal life is still practiced by many African families. (Right) A native woman weaves a souvenir to sell in a market in Mpumalanga.

5 Rainbow Nation

ARCHBISHOP DESMOND TUTU dubbed South Africa the "Rainbow Nation" to describe the diversity of people who call it their home. This rainbow metaphor recognizes all the shades of the racial spectrum. In contrast to the prevailing attitude during the apartheid era, the new South Africa celebrates the uniqueness of every ethnic or tribal group.

About three-fourths of South Africa's 42.7 million people are black. Several groups with ancient tribal heritages, such as the Xhosa, the Zulu, and the Sotho, maintain their cultural and language identities today, although they are also part of the larger black community.

Some elements of tribal life are still prevalent, particularly in the rural areas of the country. Although many of the roughly 7 million Xhosa have moved to the cities and adapted to Western culture and lifestyles, some still

Quick Facts: The People of South Africa

Population: 42,768,678
Ethnic Groups: black 75.2%, white 13.6%, Colored 8.6%, Indian 2.6%
Age structure:
  0–14 years: 30%
  15–64 years: 65%
  65 years and over: 5%
Population growth rate: 0.01%
Birth rate: 18.87 births/1,000 population
Infant mortality rate: 60.84 deaths/1,000 live births
Death rate: 18.42 deaths/1,000 population
Life expectancy at birth:
  total population: 46.56 years
  male: 46.57 years
  female: 46.54 years

Total fertility rate: 2.24 children born/woman
Religion: Christian 68% (includes most whites and Coloreds, about 60% of blacks and about 40% of Indians), Muslim 2%, Hindu 1.5% (60% of Indians), indigenous beliefs and animist 28.5%
Languages: 11 official languages, including Afrikaans, English, Ndebele, Pedi, Sotho, Swazi, Tsonga, Tswana, Venda, Xhosa, Zulu
Literacy: 86.4%

All figures are 2003 estimates unless otherwise indicated.
Source: Adapted from CIA World Factbook, 2003.

live in the Eastern Cape region, where they preserve the Xhosa tradition of cattle herding. Many still live in beehive-shaped huts and follow tribal culture and traditions. For example, as a rite of passage to adulthood, some teenage girls and boys will live away from a Xhosa village for a time. At tribal ceremonies, men and older women smoke pipes.

A large number of South Africa's 8 million Zulus live in the KwaZulu-Natal Province. While they are not untouched by modern life, tribal traditions are still highly valued by the Zulu people. Cattle herding and farming are the primary ways they make a living, although mining and tourism are also common fields of work. Some Zulu make money by selling crafts, such as pottery and beadwork. In traditional homes, boys are trained to take care of the cattle while the girls are responsible for preparing meals and doing the housekeeping. Older Zulu keep the culture alive through storytelling, dance, and song.

Many South African blacks—both Xhosa and Zulu—still practice *lobola*, a tribal custom in which the groom offers a dowry, or a price, for his bride. Traditionally, the price was paid in cattle, but today money is more commonly presented. Proponents of *lobola* say the practice demonstrates the groom's respect for the bride's family and enhances the relationships among the extended family.

Other Ethnic Groups

Whites account for about 13 percent of the South African population. Some whites are of British descent, but the majority of them are Afrikaners, whose ancestors came from Holland and France. The Dutch immigrants were typically employees of the Dutch East India Tea Company, and the French immigrants were Protestants seeking refuge from their Catholic homeland. This mix produced a distinct culture and language, Afrikaans.

Afrikaners had strong ties to the conservative Dutch Reformed Church, which later fueled much apartheid rhetoric. However, the end of apartheid did not mean the end of Afrikaner religious thinking, as most still belong to the Dutch Reformed Church. Afrikaners also still speak Afrikaans and create music and literature in the language. *Boeremusiek*, the lively, traditional Afrikaner music that features a concertina (a handheld accordion), banjo, and drums, remains popular today.

South Africans of mixed black and white heritage are known as "Coloreds." Today there are almost 4 million Coloreds living in South Africa.

In the United States, *Colored* is an archaic, offensive term that once identified blacks, but in South Africa, it is an accepted term that refers to people of black and white heritage. Today, there are about 3.8 million South African Coloreds, a large percentage of whom live in Cape Town. The primary language of the Coloreds is Afrikaans.

Indians and Chinese comprise about 2.6 percent of South Africa's population—roughly one million people. Originally, Indians were brought to South Africa as indentured servants in the late 1800s to work on sugar plantations; they worked without pay for a preestablished period of time until they were freed. The Chinese were first brought to South Africa at the turn of the 20th century to work in the mines. Today, most South African Asians live in KwaZulu-Natal.

Many People, Many Faiths

South Africa is predominantly a Christian nation, the cumulative result of missionary trips over the centuries. The majority of Afrikaners are members of the Dutch Reformed Church, but some practice other Protestant faiths or Catholicism. Tribal people who have embraced Christianity often blend it with ancient traditions, such as ancestor worship and belief in a Supreme Being.

Other major religions are observed in South Africa. The Indians who arrived to work in the sugar cane fields brought Hinduism, and approximately 600,000 Hindus still practice in South Africa today. About 650,000 South Africans practice Islam, which slaves from Asia and the rest of Africa introduced to the region. Today, there are more than 500 mosques in the country.

The Sporting Life

In South Africa, there's a sport for everyone to either cheer for or play.

About 68 percent of South Africans are Christians. Many of them are members of one of the Afrikaner churches, which are related to the Dutch Reformed Church. These include the Nederduitse Gereformeerde Kerk (NGK), the Nederduitse Hervormde Kerk (NHK), and the Gereformeerde Kerk (Doppers).

Apartheid took its toll on South Africa's athletes, because for about 30 years, they were not allowed to participate in international competitions such as the Olympics. Since the official end of apartheid, athletes have been welcomed back to the world's playing fields.

Soccer is a widely followed sport, and the most popular team is the Bafana Bafana, or "the Boys" (*bafana* is the Zulu word for "young boys.")

Bafana Bafana fans proudly support their team during an international soccer competition against Sweden, played at Loftus Versfeld in Pretoria. Soccer is one of the most popular sports in South Africa.

Bafana is among the best soccer teams in Africa, and in 1996 it won the African Nations Cup championship.

There is a decidedly British influence on the South African athletic scene. Sports fans avidly follow cricket, a distant cousin of baseball, and rugby, British-style football. Rugby had once been known as a "white man's game," but the end of apartheid has inspired efforts to make it a sport for everyone.

Outdoors enthusiasts have activities to choose from in South Africa. Swimming, surfing, and scuba diving are all popular. Mountain climbers have the Cape Fold and Drakensberg ranges to test their skills. Runners looking for all the glory try the annual 55-mile (89-km) Comrades Marathon, which goes from Pietermaritzburg to Durban.

A Wealth of Artisans

The crafts of South Africa, such as glass beadwork and basketmaking, are admired worldwide. While beadwork is considered little more than a fashion statement to some Westerners, for some tribes, such as the Zulus, it signifies a lot more. The colors of the beads and the patterns selected usually have special symbolic meanings. For example, one type of bead presentation shows that a young woman is engaged.

South Africa has produced some literary gems along with its diamonds and gold. Alan Paton, perhaps South Africa's best-known author, wrote about his racially divided homeland in the acclaimed novel *Cry, the Beloved Country*. More recently, novels, short stories, and poetry about post-apartheid issues have filled bookstore shelves. In 2003, J. M. Coetzee, an English-speaking author of Afrikaner descent, received the Nobel Prize for

Literature. Several of his novels, such as *Waiting for the Barbarians* and *Disgrace*, explore racial themes. Other writers who tackle similar issues are Nobel laureate Nadine Gordimer and Zakes Mda, a black South African author and playwright. Mda spent 32 years in exile in the United States for speaking out against apartheid.

Oral storytelling is a traditional and colorful way for tribespeople to share their legends, but there are also members of tribes who have committed their stories to paper and have gained a wide audience. Among them are B. W. Vilakazi (1907–47), who wrote his poems in the Zulu language, and Peter Mtuze, a writer and linguist who translated Nelson Mandela's 1995 autobiography, *Long Walk to Freedom*, from English to Xhosa.

South Africa's music is diverse and distinctive. Kwela jazz features the pennywhistle, and *mbaqanga*, a "township jive" dance music, became popular in the 1950s and 1960s. These styles continue to influence South African pop music today. Ladysmith Black Mambazo is a famous South African vocal group that performs **isicathamiya** music, a variation on traditional "call and response" songs. Singer/songwriter Paul Simon brought Ladysmith to the world's attention on his 1986 *Graceland* album, and the Grammy-winning vocalists have been South Africa's cultural ambassadors ever since.

Food

A favorite activity in the South Africa sun is the **braai**, a barbecue featuring **boerewors** (sausages) or steak. South Africans don't limit themselves to meats typically found in American supermarkets, but will consider ostrich, springbok (African gazelle), or crocodile burgers for dinner. The

A family holds a *braai* at a local park. Barbecued sausages are a popular food for picnics and at afternoon meals.

catch of the day could be crayfish, oysters, or yellowfish. Enthusiasts of South African–style Indian cooking eat **bobotie**, a type of curry.

A three-legged iron *potjie* pot over hot coals is the perfect way to cook *potjiekos*, a vegetable and meat stew. Other favorite dishes are salty biltong, a dried beef or venison jerky, and **samp**, a maize meal that, along with vegetables, serves as daily fare among blacks living in rural regions.

Two views of Johannesburg, South Africa's largest and most important city. (Opposite) As the modern skyscrapers of downtown Johannesburg indicate, the city has grown a great deal since being established as a mining town in 1886. (Right) Gold Reef City in Johannesburg has an underground mine and a Victorian fun fair that attract many tourists.

6 South Africa's Urban Gems

THE 42.7 MILLION people of South Africa live in the widest imaginable range of environments—from tribal villages to the most modern cities, from deep poverty to great luxury. Since the first democratic elections of 1994, several towns and municipalities have changed their names or are in the process of changing them, replacing Afrikaner names with black African ones. In order of greatest to smallest population, South Africa's major cities are Johannesburg, Cape Town, Durban, and Pretoria.

Johannesburg

People call it Joburg, the City of Gold, or simply Johannesburg. Whichever name they use, they're talking about a city rich in history with prospects for a dazzling future. In 1886, a man named George Harrison discovered gold on the Witwatersrand Main Reef, and with mining fever came the unprecedented growth of a small town. More than a century later, the small town has become a thriving city with over 5.2 million people, according to 2004 estimates.

Joburg has its fair share of museums, art galleries, and fine restaurants and shops. The Johannesburg Art Gallery proudly displays works by South African artists, such as Irma Stern, and European masters like Picasso and Rodin. Some of Johannesburg's newer landmarks are a tribute to past and present heroes. The 931-foot-long (284-meter) Nelson Mandela Bridge, which opened in July 2003, is southern Africa's largest cable-stayed bridge. It connects areas north of Johannesburg to the center city's cultural and business district and is considered to be pivotal to the city's goal of revitalization. Throughout the city, visitors can find statues of Mohandas Gandhi (1869–1948), an Indian political and spiritual leader who lived in Johannesburg and Durban during the turn of the 20th century. While he lived there, he fought to end discrimination against Indians.

Four miles south of the city is Johannesburg is Gold Reef City, where an elevator takes visitors down a mineshaft to experience what life was like for the miners a century ago. Despite the city's origins as a mining center, less than 1 percent of Johannesburg residents are employed as miners. Many people work in either retail or wholesale businesses or financial services.

Cape Town

For much of its history, South Africa's Cape Town was a well-kept secret from the rest of the world. Today, the historic and cultural riches of this city—

the oldest in South Africa—twinkle on the world's stage.

With over 3.2 million people in 2004, Cape Town is South Africa's second most populous city and its legislative center (Pretoria is the administrative capital and Bloemfontein is the judicial center). The Khoikhoi were one of the

From Signal Hill, visitors have a clear view of Cape Town, South Africa's oldest city. An historic city with a modern outlook, Cape Town often draws comparisons to San Francisco.

tribes known to have lived in this beautiful land. Explorer Bartholomeu Dias was the first white man to set eyes on the Cape region in 1488, and in 1652, the Dutch East India Tea Company formed the first settlement.

Cape Town's most familiar landmark, Table Mountain, has always been its most majestic. The flat-topped mountain, which is 3,566 feet (1,087 meters) high, rests in Table Bay; it is believed to be only one-sixth of its original height. Few of Cape Town's visitors are content to merely enjoy the view of the mountain, but must see it firsthand by hiking it.

In 1902, when Cecil John Rhodes died bequeathing Kirstenbosch as part of his land estate to South Africa, he probably had not imagined it would become one of the world's foremost botanical sites. The Kirstenbosch National Botanical Gardens, on the eastern edge of Table Mountain, is where about one-fourth of South Africa's flowering plants is cultivated.

Off Cape Town's shore is Robben Island, where Nelson Mandela was exiled. Site of a high-security prison for almost 350 years, the island is now a visitor's attraction that depicts the old South Africa during apartheid. It is also a wildlife sanctuary for seals, whales, seabirds, and other marine animals.

Cape Town is home to South Africa's Houses of Parliament. It also contains many important historic buildings: the Castle of Good Hope, dating back to the 1660s, was originally a fort, and the Groote Kerk (Great Church), a structure built in the mid-1800s, features a 6,000-pipe organ. The Bo-Kaap Museum explores the lives of the Cape Malay Muslims, slaves brought to South Africa from Singapore, Indonesia, and Madagascar.

Although Cape Town is an old city, it has a modern outlook and a bustling downtown with high-rise buildings. The city is often described as

Robben Island was once home to a high-security prison; Nelson Mandela was one of its most famous inmates. The island also served as a leper colony and lunatic asylum at different points in time.

the South African counterpart to San Francisco. There are about 40,000 businesses, most of which are in the financial and trade sectors. Other important Cape Town industries are mining, manufacturing, transportation, and construction. A revitalized harbor area, the Victoria and Alfred Waterfront, adds to the city's charm and stimulates its economy.

Durban

Durban, South Africa's third-largest city with an estimated population of 2,531,000 in 2004, is more than just a coastal beauty. Nestled along the Indian Ocean, Durban is the country's premier seaport and boasts one of the

Durban's "Golden Mile" is actually a four-mile stretch of Indian Ocean coastline. Durban is South Africa's most important seaport.

world's largest harbors. More than 4,000 commercial ships dock at the enormous Port of Durban every year.

This city has many historic, cultural, and natural sites of interest. In an unusual and dramatic turnaround, the building where blacks once were required to register is now the KwaMugle Museum, which chronicles the journey to racial equality. The Umgeni River Bird Park is for nature lovers and has more than 3,000 birds representing 400 species.

The tourism and maritime businesses account for much of Durban's economy. The city, site of an international film festival for more than 20 years, might add "movie making" to its business roster, if current efforts to promote Durban's film industry succeed.

While Gandhi lived in Durban and was practicing law, he was removed from a first-class train compartment reserved only for whites. Shortly after, he began developing his philosophy of non-violent protest. Today, most of South African's Indian population lives in or near Durban. The Alayam Hindu Temple and the Indian Market are two hallmarks of the city's Indian community.

Pretoria

South Africa's administrative capital, Pretoria, is located in Gauteng Province about 35 miles (58 kilometers) north of Johannesburg. With nearly 1.6 million residents in 2004, Pretoria is the country's fourth-largest city. It was named after Andries Pretorius, a military leader and Afrikaner hero. Pretoria's streets are lined with Jacaranda trees, which burst into lovely purple blossoms in South Africa's springtime. Some people have given Pretoria the nickname "the Jacaranda City." Its Sotho name is *Tshwane*, which means, "We are one because we live together."

Pretoria became the capital of the Transvaal in 1860. Reminders of Pretoria's past are found in and around the city today. South of the city lie Fort Klapperkop and Fort Schanskop, two stone-and-brick forts built by the Boers at the turn of the 20th century. They were later occupied by the British. Artifacts from the Great Trek are preserved in the Voortrekker Monument and Museum, and a statue of Paul Kruger, the Transvaal president, stands in Church Square.

Located in Pretoria, Church Square derives its name from a small thatched-roof Dutch Reformed church that was dedicated here in 1857. Historical buildings like the government building (known as the Raadzaal), the Palace of Justice, the old Post Office, and the Standard Bank surround the square.

Pretoria is a well-known city for many other reasons. It is home to one of the country's most prestigious schools, Pretoria University, and the State Theatre. The National Zoological Gardens is the largest of its type in Africa.

Pretoria's economy is bolstered by its status as the center of South African government, and several foreign embassies are located throughout the city. Many people have jobs in government offices or are employed in businesses that serve or support the government. Pretoria also is known as South Africa's science and technology base. Its major industries include food processing, iron and steelworks, and engineering.

Townships

Nearly every large South African city has neighboring settlements known as townships. Townships assumed their earliest form around the turn of the 20th century, when white settlers, mistakenly believing that blacks were carriers of disease, ordered them to live on the outskirts of their communities. As South Africa became more industrialized, many blacks left their villages to work in the cities. By the late 1940s, the South African government was building cheap housing to accommodate the influx of black labor. As apartheid gained support over time, National Party policy resulted in the forcible relocation of urban blacks.

Soweto (Southwest Township), near Johannesburg, is probably the most well known of South Africa's townships. It is now a city with an estimated 2004 population of 1,465,200 people (some estimates report a higher population, though a reliable census has not yet been taken.) In 1976, schoolchildren assembled to protest the government's decision to make Afrikaans the official school language; the protest turned violent, and more than 600 people were killed in what has become known as the Soweto Uprising.

Today, Soweto is South Africa's most densely populated black residential area. Visitors tour Soweto and other townships for the history and culture the neighborhoods offer. While the post-apartheid government has made efforts to improve conditions in the townships, poverty and crime are still widespread.

A Calendar of South African Festivals

January

Like many countries, South Africa likes to begin the new year with a party; with the **Coon Carnival**, the party lasts two days. **Tweede Nuwejaar**, or Second New Year (January 2), is held in Cape Town and has a festive atmosphere similar to that of New Orleans' Mardi Gras in the United States. The celebration features brightly costumed minstrels who perform through the city's streets.

March

Human Rights Day, observed on March 22, reminds South Africans that everyone's civil liberties are now protected by the post-apartheid constitution.

April

Observed on the Monday after Easter Sunday, **Family Day** is devoted to family activities. One of the country's newer holidays, **Freedom Day**, commemorates South Africa's first democratic election, held on April 27, 1994.

May

Workers' Day, observed on May 1, honors South Africa's laborers.

June

The Bantu system, which denied black South African children the right to a decent education, sparked a protest march in June 1976 that became violent. About 20,000 young people attended the event, held in Soweto. **Youth Day**, observed on the date the march began, June 16, is a tribute to the more than 600 black South Africans who died during the riots.

July

The **National Arts Festival** is held for 11 days every July in Grahamstown in Eastern Cape. About 100,000 people come to enjoy the talents of actors, musicians, dancers, and craftspeople.

August

The contributions South African women have made against apartheid are remembered on August 9, **National Women's Day**. On that same date in 1956, women participated in a national march against pass laws in Pretoria.

September

Heritage Day, held on September 24, recognizes the cultures and traditions of South Africa's many ethnic groups.

December

Under apartheid, December 16 was observed as the **Day of the Vow**. It celebrated the Voortrekkers' military victory over the Zulus in 1838. Today, December 16 is still a holiday, but now South Africans celebrate racial harmony and understanding and call it the **Day of Reconciliation.**

In mostly Christian South Africa, **Christmas** is celebrated on December 25 as the birthday of

Jesus Christ. It is similar to other Christmas celebrations in the West, with the exchange of presents, large family gatherings, and a holiday meal, though it is different in that it falls in the middle of summer instead of winter. On the **Day of Goodwill**, December 26, South Africans help the less fortunate.

Religious Observances

South African Christians observe holy days that fall on particular days each year. However, other major celebrations are held according to a lunar calendar, in which the months are related to the phases of the moon. A lunar month is shorter than the typical month of the Western calendar. Therefore, the dates for **Easter** and other celebrations vary from year to year.

Every Easter, more than a million members of the Zion Christian Church make a pilgrimage to the denomination's headquarters in the Limpopo town of Moria. The faithful gather to hear Easter sermons, but also to sing, dance, and pray throughout the weekend. By some accounts, this church festival is the African continent's largest annual religious gathering. The Zion Christian Church, the largest of the black African Independent Churches, is Pentecostal and has about 4 million members. Church members believe that physical healing can occur through the prayers of the faithful.

Recipes

Grilled Mealie Cake

1 1/3 cups cornmeal
1 cup milk
3 cups water
1 tsp. salt
1 tsp. yellow food coloring
8 oz. sweet corn, frozen or canned
4 Tbsp. butter
2 eggs

Directions:
1. Mix cornmeal with milk and yellow food coloring to a smooth paste.
2. Boil water; add salt and cornmeal paste, stirring briskly with a whisk. Reduce heat and cook slowly, stirring frequently with a wooden spoon to prevent porridge from burning.
3. After 20 minutes, add sweet corn and cook until porridge is done.
4. Remove from heat. Add butter and beaten eggs and stir until smooth.
5. Turn into a cake pan with a loose bottom. Cover with a damp towel and allow to cool and firm up.
6. Cut into wedges, brush with olive oil, and grill briefly in a frying pan to heat through.

Ginger Pudding

2 cups flour
1/2 cup margarine
1/2 cup corn syrup
1/2 cup apricot jam
4 Tbsp. ground ginger
Baking soda
Milk
1/2 cup sugar
1/2 cup water

Directions:
1. Mix together jam, butter, and corn syrup. Sift in flour and ginger.
2. Dissolve baking soda in milk and add to mixture.
3. Make a syrup by mixing sugar and water. Bring to boil until sugar dissolves and becomes golden brown. Pour syrup into baking dish, and pour the rest of the mixture on top.
4. Bake in preheated oven at 350°F for 30 minutes. Serve hot with custard.

Creamy Polenta

6 cups cornmeal
1 gallon water
4 tsp. salt
1 1/2 tsp. yellow food coloring
1 3/4 cups cream
1 3/4 cups sweetened condensed milk

Directions:

1. Bring water to boil. Add yellow food coloring and salt, then add cornmeal and mix until smooth.
2. Reduce heat and cook under lid for 40 minutes or until done, stirring occasionally.
3. Add heavy cream and sweetened condensed milk. Stir until well blended and smooth.
4. Serve with meat dishes.

Mealie Meal Pancakes

2 cups flour
2 tsp. cayenne pepper
2 tsp. flavor enhancer, such as Accent
3 eggs
3 cups milk
1 cup cornmeal
1 tsp. yellow food coloring
1 stick butter, melted
1/2 cup oil

Directions:

1. Beat eggs, milk, food coloring, and cayenne pepper together. Stir in melted butter, flavor enhancer, and cornmeal.
2. Sift flour into liquid mixture and beat until batter is smooth. Cover and let stand 30 minutes.
3. Make pancakes to desired size on griddle. Pancakes can be filled with meat or vegetables as desired.

All recipes are reprinted with the permission of Peter Hallmanns, Advisory Chef, Nestlé Food Services.

Glossary

Afrikaans—a spoken and written language developed by early Dutch, French, and German South African immigrants; linguistically, it resembles Dutch.

amnesty—a general pardon for those who have committed political crimes.

apartheid—the policy of racial segregation and white supremacy developed and implemented by the Afrikaners' National Party from the 1940s through the end of the 1980s.

bobotie—curry cooked in the South African style.

boeremusiek—lively, traditional Afrikaner music that features the concertina (a hand-held accordion).

boerewors—a type of sausage.

braai—a South African barbecue.

drought—a long period of time when there is little or no rainfall.

duty—a tax on imported or exported goods.

economic sanctions—limits on trade and business dealings that are imposed by a country to protest another's policies or actions.

isicathamiya—a style of South African music that is a variation on traditional "call and response" songs.

lobola—the tribal custom of a groom offering a dowry, or a price, for his bride.

pass books—identification documents that blacks had to carry and present to white authorities upon demand under the apartheid system.

Rainbow Nation—a nickname for South Africa that recognizes its ethnic and cultural diversity.

samp—a maize meal that is a staple of the black South African diet.

townships—predominantly black housing developments located on the outskirts of South African cities and towns.

treason—the act of betraying or being disloyal to a country.

trekboers—semi-nomadic Afrikaner farmers; the name from which the Boers derived their name.

Voortrekkers—Afrikaans for "those who move ahead," they were the *trekboers* who made the Great Trek for new land.

Project and Report Ideas

Reports

Write one-page biographies on any of the following people:

King Shaka	P. W. Botha
Stephen Biko	Archbishop Desmond Tutu
F. W. de Klerk	Nelson Mandela

Debate

A debate is a spoken presentation about two sides of an issue or idea. One person uses facts to support one side of the issue; the other debater uses facts that support the opposite side. Hold a debate on issues pertaining to South Africa in your classroom. The class can be divided in half on a particular topic. Here are some topics:

- During the 1960s, the African National Congress's fight against apartheid was like the civil rights movement in the United States.
- In recent years, there have been too many wild animals attacking cattle and sheep on South African farms. Some people argue that they should be able to hunt wild animals with no limitations; conservationists believe that these animals need to be protected.
- The post-1994 South African government has had to face the widespread problems of unemployment, crime, poverty, and HIV/AIDS. Some believe that the government has not properly tackled these problems; others believe it has done an adequate job under the circumstances.
- To make up for past wrongs, some people have proposed the solution of giving money to South Africa's tribes for the land that countries took from them hundreds of years ago.

Poster

South Africa is home to one of the most diverse and beautiful arrays of plants, animals, and birds in the world. Choose an animal, plant, or bird to paint or draw on a large piece of poster board. Next to this image, write a description of where your living thing can be found in South Africa. Be sure to include one extraordinary characteristic (speed, height, etc.) as well as information about the species' habitat. Have people helped or threatened its survival?

Television Interview

Pretend you have the power to travel through time and can interact with famous figures of the past, present, and future. Stage a 10-minute "talk show" before the class. Have famous guests discuss what life was, or is, like in South Africa, as well as important issues of their day. One student can be the host and ask the questions; two or more other students can be the interviewees. The following are possible guests to have:

- A tribal chief/white settler of the 1600s
- An Afrikaner/Briton fighting in the Anglo-Boer War/South African War (1899–1902)
- Afrikaner/African National Congress member (1960s)
- Black/White/Colored/Indian (2000)
- Black/White/Colored/Indian (2050)

Chronology

First millennium B.C.	Various peoples, including the San and Khoikhoi, inhabit modern-day South Africa.
1300–1500	The Khoisan establish chiefdoms in the southern and southwestern Cape regions.
1488	Portuguese explorer Bartholomeu Dias becomes the first white man to sight the Cape of Good Hope.
1652	The Dutch East India Tea Company forms a settlement at the Cape.
1779	The first of several frontier wars breaks out between the British and the Xhosa tribe.
1814	The British take control of the Cape from the Dutch.
1834	The slave trade is abolished.
1835–38	The Boers make the Great Trek from the Cape to South Africa's interior; the Zulu and Ndebele tribes are defeated in battle.
1869	Diamonds are discovered in Kimberley.
1881	Afrikaners defeat the British in the Battle of Majuba Hill.
1883	Paul Kruger wins election to become the first president of the new South African Republic.
1886	Gold is discovered in Witwatersrand.
1899–1902	The Anglo-Boer War, or South African War, takes place; Britain emerges victorious.
1910	The Union of South Africa is formed.
1912	The organization later known as the African National Congress (ANC) is founded.
1913	The Natives Land Act keeps blacks from owning non-tribal lands.
1918	The Afrikaner Broederbond (League of Afrikan Brothers) is established.
1948	The National Party gains political power; apartheid policy is first implemented.

Chronology

1953	The Bantu Education Act is passed, establishing segregation in schools.
1960	At Sharpeville, 67 black demonstrators are killed; the government bans the ANC.
1961	South Africa becomes a republic and withdraws from the British Commonwealth.
1963	Nelson Mandela and other ANC leaders are tried and found guilty of treason, receiving sentences of life imprisonment.
1970s	Blacks are resettled in "homelands."
1976	In June, more than 600 South Africans are killed in the Soweto student uprising.
1977	The United Nations imposes arms embargo against South Africa; resistance leader Steve Biko dies while in police custody.
1986	The United States imposes sanctions against South Africa.
1989	F. W. de Klerk is elected president of South Africa; releases several ANC prisoners.
1990	The ban on the ANC is lifted. Nelson Mandela is freed from prison.
1991	De Klerk repeals apartheid laws.
1994	Nelson Mandela is elected president of South Africa.
1996	The Truth and Reconciliation Commission begins hearings on human rights violations; a new constitution is accepted by Parliament.
1999	Thabo Mbeki is elected president of South Africa.
2002	Bombs are set off in Soweto and Pretoria; extremists are charged with plotting against the government.
2003	The government approves comprehensive HIV/AIDS program.
2004	In elections in April, the ruling ANC preserves its majority and Thabo Mbeki is re-elected for a second term.

Further Reading/Internet Resources

Clark, Domini. *South Africa: The Land*. New York: Crabtree Publishing, 2000.

Kramer, Ann. *Nelson Mandela*. New York: Raintree Publishers, 2003.

Stotko, Mary-Ann. *South Africa*. Milwaukee, Wisc.: Gareth Stevens, 2001.

Tames, Richard. *The End of Apartheid: A New South Africa*. Chicago: Heinemann Library, 2001.

Wulfsohn, Gisèle. *In a South African City*. New York: Benchmark Books, 2002.

Travel Information

http://www.southafrica.net
http://tourism.org.za/

History and Geography

http://www.geographia.com/south-africa
http://www.sahistory.org.za/

Economic and Political Information

http://www.gov.za
http://www.anc.org.za

Culture and Festivals

http://www.languages.web.za/
http://www.music.org.za/
http://www.goafrica.co.za/southafrica/arts/festivals.html

Department of Environmental Affairs and Tourism
Private Bag X447
Pretoria, South Africa
Phone: +27 (12) 310-3911
Fax: +27 (12) 322-2682
Web site: http://www.environment.gov.za

Embassy of the Republic of South Africa
3051 Massachusetts Ave., NW
Washington, DC 20008
Phone: (202) 232-4400
Fax: (202) 265-1607
Web site: http://www.saembassy.org/
E-mail: info@saembassy.org

South African Chamber of Business
24 Sturdee Avenue
Rosebank
Gauteng, South Africa
Phone: +27 (11) 446-3800
Fax: +27 (11) 446-3847/9
Web site: http://www.sacob.co.za
E-mail: info@sacob.co.za

Index

Numbers in **bold italic** refer to captions.

Index

Contributors/Picture Credits

Professor Robert I. Rotberg is Director of the Program on Intrastate Conflict and Conflict Resolution at the Kennedy School, Harvard University, and President of the World Peace Foundation. He is the author of a number of books and articles on Africa, including *A Political History of Tropical Africa* and *Ending Autocracy, Enabling Democracy: The Tribulations of Southern Africa*.

Sheila Smith Noonan is a writer from New Jersey. She has a B.A. in political science and journalism and graduated with honors from Douglass College, Rutgers University.